CREATIVE EDUCATION

JOAN ST. PETER

Published by Creative Education
123 South Broad Street, Mankato, Minnesota 56001
Creative Education is an imprint of The Creative Company

Designed by Rita Marshall
Cover Illustration by Rob Day

Photos by: Bettmann Archives, Bruce Bennett Studios, Focus on Sports,
Sports Photo Masters

Printed in the United States of America.

Library of Congress Cataloging-in-Publication Data

St. Peter, Joan.
Los Angeles Kings / Joan St. Peter.
p. cm. — (NHL Today)
ISBN 0-88682-677-2

1. Los Angeles Kings (Hockey team)—History—Juvenile literature.
[1. Los Angeles Kings (Hockey team)—History. 2. Hockey—History.]
I. Title. II. Series.

GV848.L67S76 1995 93-48432
796.962'64'0979494—dc20

123456

Miracle on Manchester

It wasn't the regular season that the Los Angeles Kings' fans and players remember about the 1981 season. It was the post-season and an incredible Kings comeback known as "the Miracle on Manchester."

The Kings finished in fourth place in the Smythe Division in 1981–82 with 63 points, good for only 17th place overall. Heading into the playoffs, it looked like it would be a short trip for the Kings as they faced the mighty Edmonton Oilers, first-place finishers in the Smythe Division and second overall. The Oilers were

The acrobatic Mario Lessard played six seasons with the Kings.

led by the young phenom Wayne Gretzky, who earlier that season had shattered the NHL record by scoring 92 goals. The stage was set for what was expected to be a first-round mismatch between the Oilers and the Kings.

1967

Real Lemieux was a top playmaker, with 23 assists and 60 penalty minutes.

In a best-of-five series, Edmonton hosted the first two games, which the teams split. With the series tied, the players headed to Los Angeles for Game 3. The L.A. Forum on Manchester Boulevard was jumping with electricity for the April 10 match as the fans filled the arena. But the sparks quickly died out as the Oilers took control and scored five unanswered goals. By the end of the second period, the game appeared to be over due to the embarrassing performance of the Kings.

But during the second intermission, the Kings somehow pulled themselves together and came back on the ice determined to play hockey. The next 20 minutes sent chills through the crowd. One goal at a time, the Kings began their uphill battle. Soon the team had scored four goals and the game was within reach at 5-4.

With a power-play advantage, the Kings pulled their goaltender for a sixth attacker. Then, with only five seconds left on the clock, Steve Bozek scored to send the game into overtime. It was an unknown Kings rookie left wing named Daryl Evans who managed to find the back of the net at only 2:15 into the extra period. After crawling out from under the pile of Kings on top of him, Evans emerged to take a victory lap, celebrating what he called "the greatest hockey moment of my life."

The fans responded to the win with a motorcade that began at the Forum and stretched down Manchester Boulevard for miles. The Kings had made an amazing comeback. What seemed impossible against Wayne Gretzky and the Edmonton Oilers has now become known as "the Miracle on Manchester."

Bernie Nicholls was a consistent performer in the 1980s *(page 7).*

CCM
Cooper
Cooper
TITAN
M2020
TITAN
CCM

In 1967 the National Hockey League doubled its size and expanded out of its eastern regional territory, becoming a truly national league. Out of "the Great Expansion" came six new NHL teams: the Los Angeles Kings, Oakland Seals, Pittsburgh Penguins, Minnesota North Stars, St. Louis Blues and Philadelphia Flyers. In Los Angeles, Kings owner Jack Kent Cooke and his staff began planning for a new arena (the Forum), while general manager Larry Regan and head coach Red Kelly developed a game plan for putting together a team.

1 9 6 8

Bill Flett (#17) led in goalscoring during the team's first season.

One of Cooke's key concerns was how well the fans would support their new team. To get fans familiar with the players, Cooke began assigning nicknames to players on the Kings roster. If a player didn't have a nickname, one was made up for him. First-year players like Bill Flett and Howie Menard became known as "Cowboy" Flett and "Mini" Menard. Eddie Joyal and Real Lemieux became Eddie "The Jet" Joyal and Real "Frenchie" Lemieux. Some players even arrived in California for the first time in costume to complement their nicknames.

Led by Flett and Lemieux, the Kings opened the season with a bang. Their first two contests were scheduled back-to-back at home, including opening night October 14, 1967, against another expansion team, the Philadelphia Flyers. Following a scoreless first period, the 7,023 fans waited until just 3:20 of the second period for center Brian Kilrea to tally the franchise's first goal, one of two he scored in the 4-2 victory. Defenseman Jacques Lemieux and left wing Ted Irvine assisted. It was another center, Gord Labossierre, who scored the Kings' game-winning goal, breaking a tie at 13:18 of the final period. The next night, the

Kings skated away with a 5-3 win over the Minnesota North Stars.

It was the beginning of a good year. Joyal and Flett led the Kings in scoring and the goaltending duo of Wayne Rutledge and Terry Sawchuk worked its magic in net. The Kings finished their first season second in the West Division with a 31-33-10 record, only one point behind the Philadelphia Flyers.

Butch Goring played in his first of twelve seasons for the Kings.

Unfortunately for the Kings, the success of the first season evolved into growing pains. The Kings struggled with 24 wins in the 1968–69 season and only 14 wins the following season. They began the 1970s with a 63-point finish and again struggled the next year with a 49-point performance. At the same time, the postseason did not bring many rewards. The team's first six years brought only two playoff berths.

The management tried to rekindle the excitement. This time it wasn't with nicknames—it was with big names. Over the next few years, the team's roster gained such talent as Gary Edwards, Harry Howell, Jean Potvin and Rogie Vachon. Vachon, who became the Kings' first superstar and first All-Star, turned into one of the league's premier netminders during his seven-year stay with the Kings.

By the 1971–72 season, the Kings had a lineup that would carry them through most of the decade. The Kings were on the rise, and their fans took notice. After averaging just over 8,000 fans in each of the first five seasons, the team's attendance shot up by 2,000 in 1972–73. The fan base kept increasing through 1977, and it was no coincidence that the team's play improved as the attendance increased. The Kings climbed from last place in the West Division in 1971–72 to second place in the Norris Division and fourth overall in 1974–75.

Marty McSorley is a top playmaker for today's Kings.

Darryl Sydor was "Best Newcomer" (with Alex Zhitnik) in 1992-93.

DIONNE EARNS HIS CROWN

1 9 7 6

Marcel Dionne began his reign as the Kings' leading scorer for eight consecutive seasons.

On June 23, 1975, the Kings signed high-scoring superstar center Marcel Dionne. Dionne played 11 years for the Kings and rewrote the team's record book. He still holds the franchise records for most goals, assists and points in a career. "Dionne brought so many things to the Kings—speed, finesse, character and credibility," Vachon said. "He was a great competitor and a great leader in the dressing room. . . . He hated to lose. As a matter of fact, he was very disappointed he had to leave the Kings without bringing a Stanley Cup championship to L.A."

Dionne became the Kings' first player to score 50 goals and 100 points in a season and finished second in the NHL's scoring race three times. In 1979–80 he captured the league's scor-

ing crown, edging out an 18-year-old rookie named Wayne Gretzky. Although both players had the same number of points (137), Dionne received the trophy because he scored more goals. But the bond tying Gretzky and Dionne together didn't end with the 1980 scoring race. The young Gretzky found Dionne to be an inspiration. "I remember the first few games I played against him [Dionne]. He wished me good luck, talked to me . . . he really helped me," Gretzky recalled.

1983

After just one season with the team, Terry Ruskowski was selected captain.

Dionne's linemates also received much attention as "the Triple Crown Line" was born. Named for the crown on the front of the team's jersey, the line was made up of Dionne at center, Charlie Simmer on the left side and Dave Taylor on the right. Taylor, who once played on the team's fourth line, moved up to Dionne's line following an injury to another player. Taylor went on to play 14 seasons with the Kings and eventually won the NHL's Masterton and King Clancy awards for his sportsmanship. Simmer was recalled from the minor leagues to complete the winning combination. In 1980 the Triple Crown Line combined for a team record that still stands: 146 goals and 182 assists for 328 points. That year, each of the three collected over 100 points and all ranked among the top eight scorers in the league.

The individual and team successes during Dionne's tenure enabled the Kings to contend with the best teams in the league. Through the mid- and late 1970s, the Kings never finished below third in their division, finishing second four times and third twice. Dionne and Vachon, who were responsible for much of the team's success during this time, were recognized years later for their accomplishments when the Kings retired their numbers. Vachon, whose No. 30 was hoisted to the rafters in 1986, called it the most memorable day in his career. "I'll never forget the night the Kings retired my jersey. It's the ultimate honor in any sport. . . . It meant everything to me," he said. Dionne's No. 16 was retired four years later in 1990.

1 9 8 4

Pat Quinn became head coach and led the team to their first winning season since 1981.

Changes Ahead

In the early 1980s, the Miracle on Manchester, in which the Kings came from behind to defeat the Oilers, was a definite highlight. Not even their subsequent loss to the Vancouver Canucks could tarnish the memory of that great moment. But for the few seasons following, the team couldn't revive itself. They slumped to last place in the division. Despite the presence of top players such as captain Terry Ruskowski, young prospect Bernie Nicholls and the members of the Triple Crown Line, the Kings could not get their game together. Goaltending was shaky and management was criticized. By 1984, the need for a change was apparent. Pat Quinn took over as coach and Rogie Vachon returned to the Kings as general manager.

Vachon's return marked a new milestone in his career—and in the Kings' history. Once named the team's most inspirational player, Vachon now had the task of rebuilding the Kings. Under his guidance, things slowly began to take shape for the franchise. The Kings showed improvement in the regular season and finally moved out of the Smythe Division cellar. But perched on top of the division was the NHL's newest dynasty, the Edmonton Oilers. In both 1986 and 1987, the Kings dropped first-round series to Edmonton, which by now was led by some of the best hockey players in the world—Gretzky, Jari Kurri, Paul Coffey and Esa Tikkanen, to name just a few.

Wayne Gretzky is hockey's greatest scorer of all time *(page 15).*

JOFA
99
TPM2020

The Kings' frustration in the playoffs was eased by the excitement of the young, up-and-coming team that had now been assembled. In 1986–87, skilled rookies and a high-scoring defense combined to form a core that would spark the Kings for years to come. Forwards Luc Robitaille and Jimmy Carson and defenseman Steve Duchesne all made their rookie debuts for the Kings. Robitaille became the Kings' first Calder Trophy winner as the NHL's best rookie in 1987 and went on to become one of the league's highest-scoring left wings. Duchesne became the Kings' first defenseman to score 20 goals in one season.

1 9 8 4

Bernie Nicholls played an important role in the Kings' plan to rebuild.

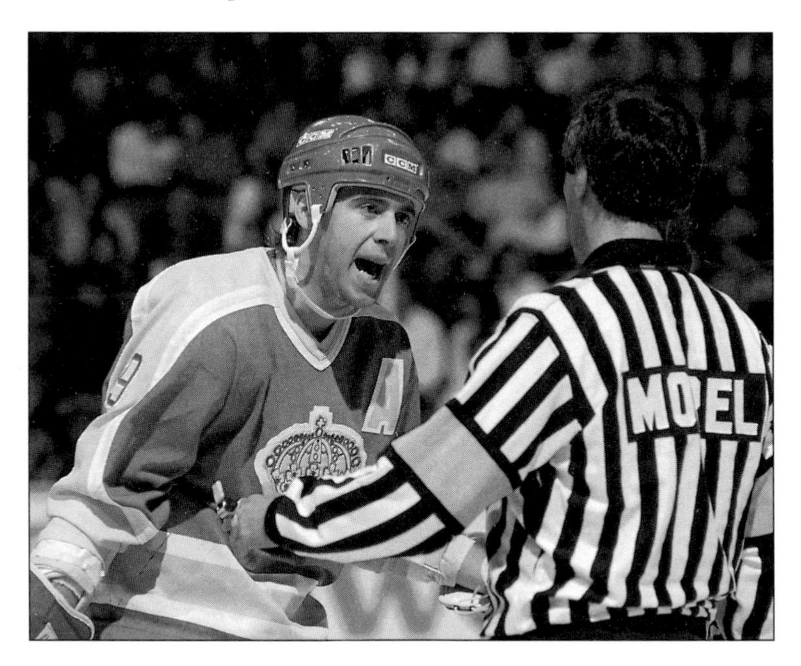

Dave Taylor played for 17 seasons in Los Angeles.

KINGS
CCM
VAUGHN
VAUGHN
VAUGHN
VAUGHN

40
40

The Kings had a taste of success, but were eager to take the next step. And, in 1988, they did just that. With the addition of one player, the Kings took not a step, but a leap, toward the next level.

Before joining the Kings, Luc Robitaille was Canadian Major Junior Player of the Year.

GRETZKY CROWNED A KING

In March 1988, Bruce McNall became sole owner of the Los Angeles Kings. Under the new ownership, things changed quickly for the team. The first change marked the end of the purple-and-gold uniform. McNall introduced a new logo and changed the team colors to a more marketable black, silver and gray. But his most spectacular decision was a trade that shook the sports world and changed southern California hockey and the NHL forever.

On August 9, 1988, all eyes were on Los Angeles as the Kings announced that the greatest hockey player of all time, Wayne Gretzky, was now a cornerstone of their team. Throngs of reporters from the United States and Canada gathered at a Los Angeles press conference to witness the news that changed the direction of the NHL. The expensive, controversial trade brought Wayne Gretzky to Los Angeles from Edmonton, where he had helped the Oilers win five Stanley Cup championships and turn the team into a dynasty. The reporters watched as Gretzky, known around the world as "The Great One," pulled on a Los Angeles Kings jersey with the new logo and new colors. That afternoon he vowed to bring the Stanley Cup to the Kings. "It would be the greatest moment in my life to bring the Stanley Cup to L.A.," Gretzky told reporters.

Jimmy Carson led the team in goal-scoring for the second consecutive season.

The team's future brightened as Gretzky, Mike Krushelnyski and Marty McSorley came to Los Angeles for Jimmy Carson, Martin Gelinas, first-round draft picks in the 1989, 1991 and 1993 drafts, plus cash estimated at $15 million. Cliff Fletcher, then the general manager of the Calgary Flames, summed it up best when he told the press that "the Kings franchise has struggled for its due recognition and credit for 21 years of its existence. Now it has it." Hockey in California was reborn.

Gretzky Reigns

Gretzky's first year at Los Angeles proved to be full of personal and team milestones. The milestones began in his opening night debut when he tallied the team's first goal of the 1988–89 season. Five games later, on October 15 at Edmonton, Gretzky passed Gordie Howe as the NHL's all-time leading scorer with his 1851st point. In his first year as a King, Gretzky earned his

Bob Kudelski joined with Gretzky to help the team rebuild.

ninth Hart Trophy as the NHL's most valuable player and finished second in the scoring race with 168 points. But the best thing that Gretzky did for his new team and fans was to bring the hope of winning a Stanley Cup to the Los Angeles Kings.

Veteran Paul Coffey brought his tough style of defense to the team.

The Kings improved over the next few years, including an immediate climb from fourth place to second in the division in Gretzky's first year. Fittingly, they faced the Oilers in the first round of the 1989 playoffs. In what is known as the second-best comeback in club history, the Kings demonstrated that a changing of the guard was taking place. After falling behind three games to one in the seven-game series, the Kings came back to win the next two, forcing a seventh game at Los Angeles. Gretzky, demonstrating why he is called The Great One, led the Kings to a victory, knocking off the defending Stanley Cup champions.

The following season, the Kings finished a disappointing fourth in the division, but Gretzky led the league in scoring with 142 points. In the first round of postseason play, the Kings defeated the defending Stanley Cup champion Calgary Flames in six games. Although L.A. lost to Edmonton in the next round, this postseason marked the second consecutive year the Kings knocked off the defending Stanley Cup champs.

The Kings began the 1990s with more success. In the 1990–91 season, Gretzky won the league's top-scorer honors again and the Kings broke the 100-point mark for the first time ever with 102 points to finish third overall. A team-record 46 wins helped them earn their first division title. The Kings went through two rounds of the playoffs, beating Vancouver in six games before losing to Edmonton in the division championship. The next season, the team performed well, finishing second in the division. But for the fifth time in seven years, the Edmonton Oilers dashed the Kings' hopes for a Stanley Cup.

Left to right: Tomas Sandstrom, Gary Shuchuk, Robb Stauber, Darryl Sydor.

Still, anticipation marked the 1993 regular season. Changes had been made to the team, such as the addition of 36-year-old head coach Barry Melrose. The roster was improved through offseason acquisitions, including Gretzky's former Oiler teammates—Jari Kurri and Paul Coffey. Optimism was running high until Gretzky suffered a herniated disc in his back that would keep him out of the lineup indefinitely. The news shocked the hockey world and rumors of The Great One's impending forced retirement plagued the Kings and the NHL. "The greatest ambassador to hockey" was in extreme pain and doctors were not sure when, or if, he would return to play the sport he loved.

1 9 9 1

Marty McSorley had the second highest PIM, the only season from 1989-93 he didn't lead the team.

"Indefinitely" turned out to be the first 39 games of the season and Gretzky returned to the ice for the second half of the season. The Kings, who had played inspired hockey in his absence, finished strong with 39 wins and 88 points, good for third place in the division.

Journey to the Cup

The 1993 postseason took the Kings on a journey they would never forget. In 26 years, the team had never advanced past the second round of the playoffs. This year there was not only a division championship, but a conference championship—and an unforgettable trip to the Stanley Cup finals.

The Kings opened the first round by defeating the Calgary Flames. Round 2 brought a matchup with the regular-season division champion Vancouver Canucks. In another close series, the teams were tied at two games apiece going into Game 5 at Vancouver. It was the first overtime game of the playoffs for Los

"The Great One," Wayne Gretzky (pages 26-27).

99
CCM
Supra

Angeles and it turned into the team's longest overtime game ever. Through the first 20 minutes of overtime, the opponents remained deadlocked at three goals apiece. But 6:21 into the second overtime, rookie Gary Shuchuk scored one of his two postseason goals to give Los Angeles the 4-3 win.

1 9 9 2

Jari Kurri scored his 500th goal vs. Boston, the 18th player to reach that milestone.

Two nights later, they went on to win the series in front of their hometown fans. The Kings had broken their playoff jinx, finally earning a conference championship berth. A Campbell Conference championship match against the Toronto Maple Leafs now awaited them.

The series began in Toronto and the Kings split two games before heading back to Los Angeles, where they split two games again. With the series tied, all eyes were fixed on Toronto for Game 5. In another close game, Glenn Anderson scored to give Toronto the series lead. Facing elimination, the Kings returned to Los Angeles for Game 6. Gretzky's total domination led the Kings to victory, including the game-winning goal at 19:20 of the overtime period. On May 29, Los Angeles beat the Leafs in Toronto 4-2 to advance to the Stanley Cup finals.

"I don't think I ever got more satisfaction than I did in winning this series," Gretzky said after the conference championship. Toronto general manager Cliff Fletcher told the press that "the greatest player in hockey beat the Leafs tonight."

But after earning the right to compete for the Stanley Cup championship, the Kings were unable to overcome the strength of the mighty Montreal Canadiens, who defeated the Kings in five games to win their 24th Stanley Cup.

Following the defeat, Kings coach Barry Melrose eased the pain a little when he told the media, "These are the best of times and these are the worst of times. . . . It's the worst of times because we lost and it's the best of times because I've been blessed with a group of players who played their hearts out."

1 9 9 3

Winger Tony Granato set career highs in assists (45) and points (82).

Heirs to the Throne

As memorable as the 1992–93 campaign was, the following season was as forgettable. The team finished with a dismal 27-45-12 record and 322 goals-against—the third highest in the league. L.A. missed the playoffs for the first time since 1986–87. But there were a few bright spots during the 1993–94 season, such as Wayne Gretzky scoring his 802nd goal and passing Gordie Howe as the league's all-time leading goalscorer. Gretzky also led the league in scoring for the 10th time in his career.

Alex Zhitnik is one of the Kings' keys to future success.

In 1994, Kelly Hrudey was the team's "Unsung Hero."

Heading into the second half of the 1990s, the Kings underwent many changes intended to turn the team around. The front office gained stability as owner Bruce McNall sold 72 percent of the team for $60 million to telecommunications executives Jeffrey Sudikoff and Joseph Cohen, and general manager Nick Beverly was replaced by Sam McMaster. On the ice, longtime Kings cornerstone Dave Taylor retired and veteran Michel Petit was added to the defensive corps. Players such as Rob Blake, Marty McSorley, Darryl Sydor and Alex Zhitnik have the potential to carry the team for years to come. And, of course, Gretzky will again lead the offensive attack.

1 9 9 5

The Kings need another strong year from Robb Stauber, who had a .908 save percentage in 1993-94.

With the new injection of excitement from the front office and the mix of talent the Kings have assembled, Wayne Gretzky's dream of landing the Stanley Cup in Los Angeles may not take long to fulfill.